Arnold Jansen op de Haar

The Refrain of Other People's Lives

Translated by John Irons

Holland Park Press London

Published by Holland Park Press 2017

First published in Dutch as *Het refrein van andermans leven* by Holland Park Press in 2016

A CIP catalogue record for this book is available from The British Library.

ISBN 978-1-907320-72-9

Cover designed by Reactive Graphics

Printed and bound by
CPI Group (UK) Ltd, Croydon CR0 4YY

www.hollandparkpress.co.uk

Isn't everyone the 'refrain of other people's lives'? This collection has to do with the feeling that your own life is determined by other people.

Arnold Jansen op de Haar (1962) moved from Arnhem to London in 2014. His emigration brought everything into focus. The poems of this collection combine to form a story. What makes somebody the person he is?

What do you do when everyone has disappeared and you are the last one?

Arnold Jansen op de Haar, shuttling between two countries, sets out in search of his history.

at my birth
my own father called me
son and heir for later
but later is last

I am the refrain of
other people's lives
I repeat a self-evident truth

The unexamined life is not worth living

Socrates

CONTENTS

AN ORDINARY DAY

such a day starts off
with yesterday's meatloaf

in a dream last night
your parents were still alive

around ten you consider
various forms of suicide

hear how veiled women are talking
underneath the colonnades

with magical eyes
and their softly voiced shisha pipe

(one can of course walk
oneself a tiny bit randy)

the drab-grey library in paddington
is meanwhile nice and warm

you think of your love
in the country where you once lived

and how she would like to have two men
or do it on public transport

or specially for you
in gleaming snug-fit

tonight you'll dream
once more of your parents

you must protect them from something
but don't know what

FIRST NAME 'I'

you are the man you have
long since become

no longer the youth
from the lean years
of ferriferous smoked meat

but of the hot plate
that quivering quavering
breeds fat folds of flab

in this house that never sees visitors
where there has been no loving

your hand that on paper
turns down the town

against the window the chippings
of fictional characters

you are an accessory to no one
but the first name 'I'

the breathing of nicotine walls
has appropriated the hours
behind the buckling wallpaper

the tableware that has fallen into disuse
the length and breadth of the night
the knife that makes soft scratches

the whetstone of two feet
under the skin of the carpet

there the fibbing
of truth began

the soft-falling rain
of recollection
onto the crackled land

the one you were accumulates
in young shoots

somewhere the questions and days
grow rampant
as if time accelerates

and when the crops
reach your lips

the nervous doubt
between countries
blossoms as spring
grows hard as winter

the harvesting comes
with the sharpness
of machines

MERCILESS RECALLING

sometimes you think of things
that have been thrown away
during hasty removals
been passed on   put in storage

that table from their wedding days
a lamp   furniture
that forgets nothing

perhaps it is a deficiency
there for generations –

a longing to retain
an ancestral whispering

sometimes you think
all that ever was
is a midwife toad
inflated with a straw

perhaps you stood there too
and did something   or laughed

or do not know why
you already see the past
in the present day

the children with their
newly acquired medals
and then in their bedside tables
seventy years later
among hankies with
initials the recovered
small box

like children sometimes
have an imaginary friend

outside the sound of
scaffolding all around
the blows of hammers
as if someone still wants
something to be done

let us begin at the beginning

now   the word meat has
become a trifle scarcer
on account of my half-vegetarian
hostess

somewhere in space
my limitless little texts are being read

I must stop using all those
diminutives

nelson's *little* column
indestructible
like *little* tweed jackets

among the children
with their *little* straw hats   I think it's
my mother's birthday but she's dead

there the park goes for a walk
the neat and tidy park
with the imaginary dog
that I will call harry
the name of a dead person
from before I was born

must one give one's dogs
the names of princes?

and at night by black light
I text on request
various ways of screwing
as a sport

I repeat words as a drill
my prick is my god

but now that I'm talking to you
let us begin at the beginning

at night my former hometown lights up
I dare to tell her
what normally one only
assumes in dreams

the words that hang
between said and unspoken

where's the nostalgia
for sadder days?
weighted with stones in the water
virginia's coat

have I already written to you:
my collarbones have
been locked for days

the flight of stairs here has been
chemically cleaned

are you still there?
for you know
let us begin at the beginning

my box files stand unsteadily
precariously like a girl's stilettos under
chalk-white legs on their way to work

I eat even the core
of the peeled past
my heart skips a beat
I get deafer by the day
decay is already setting in

perhaps you should revitalise me
in the holidays

razor blades here are a
good deal cheaper

I've just seen a van
with nsb* on it
specialist in steel doors

I must forget the euphemistic
song of my mother tongue

soon I will search for words
like the names of former female teachers

the kind of schoolmistress who brings bananas
when you are faking it

somewhere all life is raging
unto dust you will return
but what to do in the meantime?

* Nationaal-Socialistische Beweging, Dutch Nazi Party

you only get to learn a language
by saying the saying
so this is as plain as
a pikestaff
and try translating that

only when one makes the city one's own
does it offer protection

I still quietly cheer on
the dutch football team
at their midnight game

emigration   emigrants
do me a favour
like a child on a bike
look no hands
oh yes? – you still read
dutch papers

go and drink coffee with
an old jewish poet
who wed two
lapsed catholics in america

and listen   *I was in vienna*
in search of the escape
of my parents
I had just been born and
how murky that city was

at my birth
my own father called me
son and heir for later
but later is last

I am the refrain of
other people's lives
I repeat a self-evident truth

there will still be feast days
with red scrapple
asparagus and a chin
dripping with butter

I have lost everyone
and would be rid of no one

I sit like a caretaker
for the dead
among their effects

for years I have been inheriting
graves

I even so as
to save money wear
my father's shoes

on the other side of the water
lies the purloined house

home is like provisions
that you take with you unnoticed

are you coming now?
I can't say anything yet

I sleep lightly
in adjoining rooms
it will all sort itself out

let us begin at the beginning
how I have come to be here

MERCILESS LOVING

that day at departure you were
not at the station

under a scouring wind
clouds torn in tatters
and a watery sun
I stood submerged
among the chit-chatting
of tea-sipping ladies
the wishes for a good journey &
the listlessness of mouse-grey
day trippers
their mouths full of
bread and cheese

the question was: did I
because of you become one of them?

there was some time
still to be wasted

I missed the cold fire
of your eyes and the tides
of your sea

most of it was what had been
and never come into being

let us apportion the
unborn children
smash our hours
to
smith-
er-
eens

I travelled to the *monsignor* in london
who quoted socrates
the unexamined life is not worth living

before I'd even got home
everything had been written down

LONDON CALLING

now that I have avoided
major repairs like the dentist
I live for the hour on call

I must break a wall
of people
depart nonetheless

across the bank
of the guarding river
and bound for nowhere

as in a film role the windows
of the train fly past
through my birthplace

the roofs steam together
the mist falls audibly
at the department store a band
of monkeys plays jazz
in my muffled past

in brabant the stations
form a soft string of
bustling

get on   get off
get on   get off

music and friends
follow you everywhere
just as something announces itself

the sound of rivets
on a passing bridge

the graffiti stand gruffly
a thought like a dog that's broken loose –
like street litter

in dull-grey roosendaal the
low sky writes letters
on diabetic silos

the boys wolf down kebab
as if gasping for air
the girls drink diet coke

until the spring
denuded trees keep
as a memory their nests
you and I

far off roses stand on a grave

it is travelling after the event
thinking of a smoking compartment
along with your father and mother

have I said too much
stayed silent too much
fine-meshed like the rain

in mechelen I read
on a school building
thomasmore.be

travel soon
to your utopia

behind topsy-turvy houses live
other even topsy-turvier houses
abbeys   beer breweries
behind the triptychs in the churches
people are making love

it is november and stone-cold
outside brussels-south station someone
is wearing flip-flops
someone is checking an empty can of beer

someone asks for a light
someone asks the way
someone hurries homewards
someone takes his first holy communion
at the european union
someone saves a whale
with a placard
someone cooks in digs

dogs are on patrol
bound between mirror towers
in the final light

let us conquer the
shadowland

brussels lies down at night
like a war invalid with
one leg

there I stand
without belt and braces
as one condemned
in a row
and in the hall the warm opulence
of soft diamonds

no one here sees that I'm sitting
penniless

welcome to the eurostar
the bar will be opening
in 10 minutes' time

passengers walk unsteadily
in the aisle

this is the last train
a breviary
on polystyrene wheels
where people spy on each other
under the gleaming skin of displays

in the roll-down shutter landscape
the villages lie like star systems
along streets of cobblestones

heated houses
scream in the wind
and the mills turn

let us melt the freezing cold
in all languages

let us desire
catch the light in
wet furrows

beyond lille trenches
creep in the dark
the cattle stand in draughty barns
between spinneys like
phantom soldiers

everything is abandoned here
god has turned no light on

on to the heavily armed
station of calais-fréthun
and behind it teeth-chatteringly
thin the wood

deep in the earth
I think of my publisher
who taught me to walk very early –
taught me to read

in the window my
closed eye eyes
my self-portrait

above at sea
time after time
a cold front passes
everyday weather

let us now confront
cancer   reject heart failure

somewhere below along the coast
a harbour
lies warm and secure

the wheels scrape
through the garish light
of an industrial area

a tall bridge forms
an anthracite rainbow

I smell london
in the evening

with the russian girls
of tar
in inflammable streets
and furious female hair

with the gentleman in the lounge
of russell hotel who only
loves vodka and chinese women
you know   it's their buttocks

the widows' small dogs
with widowers' eyes

and at the corner shop
mr patel who says to a
lady   *no man   no wife   no life*

I must get her
to laugh right away
like a child   I think

and when the train worms
its way beneath a cast-iron sky
into st pancras

having the nerve

POET

one day he declares
his stolen memory

a long long time ago
when everything was still fine
there was a dream
of boats   the sea
and mother's potpourri

and a wax-polish-knee
that's landed in a tin
of wax polish

these are loose notes
from the section he still has

can't you recover everything here
such as love without
question?

the expanse of the universe
lies amongst the tiniest parts
of your body –
as in your memory

it is the alleged red lead
that gets in under nails
just as moisture gets into chinks

the ivy of forgetting
that deafly orders the future

DAILY WORK

this was once
– a lifetime ago –
a wretched room

on the gallery one can smell
between anvil and hammer
the ash of his house

home is the keynote

the grit of respite
jacketed by the walls

during the day he cheerfully
smears syrup round their mouth
with hands of water

but at night he is
– when in the depths
the sea demons rumble –
a rudderless submarine captain

depth charges are dropped

in the morning everything floats
to the surface
oh   the cheery office
workers   get cracking!

in the street a rattling
carcass clatters

people know where we live
someone saves his skin

what if you were to know all
that you no longer know?

every drop of rain
every sudden shower
and all the faces
of each year's class

insane my birthplace
where everyone lives
in limitless knowledge

would I recognise myself?
am I still the
one I was?

I call back hardest
the people who
disappeared first

what did he say then?
what did her voice sound like?

it has to do with genes
active for generations
mother's eyes
father's hands

anchored by threadbare templates
the crackleware of years
standing on fragile legs

the misleading past
of repeated stories

or blown away in the sight
of the storm

like bottom refers
to depth and ship

somewhere someone is keeping
everything secret

the hinges of creaking doors
to the house where
the furniture is still silent

the snapped thread and
the clicking of rolling pearls
this instance
on the ground

the mouth that distorts
deeper into furrows

I increasingly rely on
my belly in anticipation

there in the delta
black dogs slake their thirst

where are the people
who knew all about me?

LONDON VIEW

the summer gardens dream
of coolness in the listless evening air

without solace there is soon panic
the bird-sick windows
with faces on fire

the white of the house fronts
the sun that yet one more time
polishes itself in mirrors

the hour is unending

the street flakes off like birchwood
even the houses slough their skins

the child on the scooter is at the corner
calling parents   a car that hoots

the chorus of police sirens
drags snail trails in my ears

the clouds turn without a clock
the day with its parched throat
the aftertaste of water
it already smells of rain
pitch-black roads
and bare feet in the grass

shadows stand with knocking knees
like dizzy spells of aged aunts

gulls that hang screeching
in an everlasting wind

suddenly the rain lectures a child
repeats itself   repeats itself

people even live in the dankness
of basements

further up the council estate darkly lies
in post-war bombsites

a snake swishes dizzyingly
through layers of soil
the humming top of days

every hour 4000 rats are born

the light falls audibly on target
the half-full glass
splinters on the paving stones

statues of horsemen
and admirals on pillars
shiver with spears of rain

outside the city there are fields
where soldiers sleep uneasily

obscure animals scrape
their hooves

at night they toss and turn   the initiated
for diseases still to come
and changes in the weather

I look at the diorama box of rooms
on stones in which the warmth
still recalls the south side

one sits suppressing one's name
the iron spirits
ensured against loss
rusty reasons

someone uses his lips to form
an o at the window

the aeolian harp produces
ultrasonic sounds

the reptilian brain creaks

peace is never predicted
though the end of days is

on the opposite side live
those disinherited by ancestors

only old men have specialised
in genealogy

in the rooms with the harsh light
nobody is at home

a man slinks exposed
past his windows

the hunger of foxes
in mid-street

there someone is wrapping up his soul
moving house with his load

two people embrace
in perfect silence

everywhere heads are burying themselves
in pillows
with teeth of tar
from a paucity of fire-spewing spit

then the lights of taxis go out
I am one step removed
the sad necessity of life
it's not long until the chestnuts are roasted

if I had to imagine a land
I would first look for a stubborn misunderstanding
build low-lying land out of sandbanks
send a ship with cod-liver oil
I would give the land scales
against the rain
from the driftwood of history
I would fish slaves
ships   spices
collaboration and a touch of resistance
the syllables in their language
I would scrape into one guttural
in the south I would let them speak more softly
sow shoots of derision in the fields
I would give the men wooden heads
and let the women walk
as if kicking at long skirts
I would look for animals to add
that fit the bellowing wind
I would send them soothing speakers
pacifying preachers
and demonstrations for a cent
with barrel organs I would grind
their brains dry
their rivers I would let stream
as a monotonous symphony
I would give them thoughts like tides
let the wind scythe in one direction
of all isms I would give them
chauvinism
and perhaps give them
a monarchy
one night I would steal away
like a peat-moor fire

inundate the land as homesickness
with the grit of their dreams
that silts up tidal inlets

IN A TOWN LIKE THIS

one puts on one's best
city face

one congratulates oneself
on the variety of shops
on cookies like
girls made of sugar
in a tin and
– not forgetting –
the events
working-class precincts
parks
trolley buses

one praises oneself for
surrounding green areas

behind the push moraine
lie stag-bellowing crown estates
with resting places for big game

towards the south a vista
of three quarters sky

one warms oneself with the orchestra
that in a raspingly high-ceilinged room
plays free of charge at lunchtime
for those on in years

one fondly imagines
dance of international fame
and a station made of lego

appropriates
two slender youngsters
who went into fashion

round the coffee vending machines
one stands talking
about a local resident
in a talent scouting

behind shopfronts
of plastic chains
showers sweep across older land

it is not that one builds
on the shoulders of giants
but on their feet of clay

looking for something to prevent forgetting
one praises the morning
and the evening light

one thinks
CARPET-BOMB IT

IN THIS TOWN

my books have
remained in exile
a cardboard sarcophagus of data
signed on the inside cover

full of smoke and in storage
the colours faded as those of
badly clad fellow countrymen overseas

like pastry from the right shops
like sunday lunch mother wine
like meeting her in
the middle of town
in unexpected places
like a homeless person who waits for her
on sundays after church

like the mist above the river
or fireworks   clouds
yes evening light

like phoning that you're safely home
the silence of the city at night

like guts gurgling with bacillophobia
after visits to restaurants

like an aunt laden
with cheap jewellery
put her on four wheels
and simply drive off

like wild leftish nieces
turned bourgeois
who you were secretly in love with
and their absconded husbands

like talking about who
were there before you

like the visiting of the dead
on the anniversaries of their death and
at easter yellow ribbons
on their graves

like the first meeting
with the blond and grey lady
like the searching for a
dog gone astray

like smoking together
in the water meadows
or drawing animals on a
bare back with your salty fingers

or still knowing everything
about all the photos
and continuing to pass it on
to yourself

till you're just the only one
till someone opens the boxes

PRINCESSES OF PORTOBELLO

in deathly quiet streets
that speak
in stiletto-heel vowels
princesses wake up
their laudable lips
in ineffable red

in the office
with the hardwood benches
the street lots are drawn

there the iron stalls arrive
twisted by men
with callous hands

the toothpaste smile
with the paper flower
in her hair
the married couple with english crockery
a parade of dazzling-white vans
on hangers the jackets with skulls

the mother of luxury knitwear
says   *she's just finished university*

something perfect from
before the plastic era
the cheerfulness of the sixties
with suitable accessories

on the ever-windy square
with spanish-speaking windows
the clocks turn

it is snowing midsummer pollen
the sky speaks of birds
one decks oneself with
the trace of the pigeons

around midday
the yearning masses rush
round the stalls like beacons

the fear for the toddler
who strays from its parents

someone asks for
the film-star address of
extendable pastel-shade houses
a second takes snaps
of the female busker
who screws up languages
a shrieking *elvis*
insults terraces
what's this any good for?

no one says a needless goodbye
every meeting is coincidence

then the imaginary end
of the afternoon approaches
on ever slower clocks

I still have to
sell the words as silverware
to princesses

LETTER FROM EDINBURGH

it's midsummer and outside
people hide in their creaking
collars and jackets of bronze

here sounds the guttural
borrowed language from throats of
strict stone houses

visit the dead
underground

the gruffness that frowns
as where I came from
– my accent saves me –

in alleys   on squares and streets
the hand of the highlands waves

as if soon someone drives
his otherworldly sheep
into the city with dogs

angels rip the clouds open
with arrows

behind frayed ends
the dazzling green
of ancient mountains

the wear-eager rocks
of granite and basalt

the graffiti of gods

this dream landscape of elves
and giants

this is no city
this is a pre-ruin ruin

the flaming tongue
of the sinking sun
licks proud pillars

on the volcano the king sleeps
with lady macbeth in his arms

bricked up in the walls
the smell of entrails

at night someone revolves
the monuments like a clock

the wind howls in unison
with bagpipe music

the rain sputters like clattering weapons

behind the mountain ridge the four riders
of the apocalypse are galloping

this capital of homesickness
this black-scorched athens
before the storm

I dream of the whitewashed south
where under the open skies
under the open skies the sun

this is where poets
are born

HIGHGATE CEMETERY

sometimes on fine days
comrades are still carried as
pebble stones to the rock

they then lie without a doubt
grouped round their god marx
as hard core apparatchiks in
the rules of the creed

their pride in headstones
inscribed with *filmmaker*
architect or *socialist*
and mother to the end

the visitors wear beards
a cold wind gets up
amongst the stylised decay

the light falls like a guillotine

the skewed drooping graves
of the forgotten bourgeoisie
overgrown like the paths
of the gulag archipelago

the shrubs will quickly
bear bitter fruit once more
and the days lengthen
fill my cup to the brim

tell how pavlik morozov
stood before his father   denounced
him with lifted hand
and became a hero in his land

but (as if I hear my own father)
perhaps someone lies here too who
fought against the nazis or wrote
angry letters to the people's commissar

ah damned of the earth
may you rise from the dead
with your councils and committees
manifestoes and dialectical theories

oh most vain of comrades
unite once more as one
very last internationale
at highgate cemetery

MEANWHILE ON THE HOME FRONT

I already thought that days would come
when nothing would occur

the fringe
of a rusty memory

that is past

at night the black dog comes
the hordes that ask
if you can live off writing

they will say
that I've grown fatter

mark decay with your teeth
in the stones

what counts are the words   counted
and then released

along the railway track trees rustle
the wheels chafe

look into the gaping gob
of the given moment

if only no one happens to phone
no one crushes the glass underfoot
and parties afterwards

here it's raining sweat
over there peace is breaking

the city
the velvet-soft gag
at the end of the street
as a greeting   as a rule

the reckless rustling of silence
I still have to un-everyday things

over there my mother is sitting
in a chair by the window
with the same eyes
under the same sky

ANGEL

that autumn day the trees stood
with their ears laid back

the air smelt of earth

the disruptive raging
of birds
someone puts the axe to my roots

evening falls repeatedly
the half-drunken night

then the city is hurrying homewards

from empty offices
a night watchman's light shines
on the tight-throat city

you are my angel
I am not free
the broken-winged one

I resist the self-hatred
of post-war children

the angel is my father
the angel is my mother

I do not know my own limits
I live from excess

the peaceful clock hands
. that grind hours

on my balcony an olive
tree grows in frosty weather

sometimes I borrow their wings
sometimes I plunge down

I owe myself something

in a youth of ironed sheets
the fold

and summers of vest and cereal

one says *loo* and *icebox*
the right words
are very important

my father made
peace out of war

and good is a word
much too big

at times it sits stuffed in
simple people

at times in immensely rich rooms

but bad everywhere
as
in yourself

my mother always wishes me
for later
a girl like herself

mother   neighbours don't matter

dying she heats
the soup that I made

to others I say that
she can still do everything herself

and always the guilt
of being present too little

the track of a wound
in the land

the flight has begun

THE CYCLING JEWELLER

saws her rings
off ever thickening fingers
– doctor's orders –

the circles ever smaller
the eyes ever dimmer
the silent closeness
ever nearer

at eye-height the family
pass on chairs
and a rabbit
behind the settee

two weeks later
oblique on the edge of the bed
in a perpetual pose
with as a dripping tap
leaky legs   bandaged
I say that we have
carried it off
to the end

each time the house
more denuded of furniture –
she disappears through windows

so I am talking to thin air

the lamented summer
and even more the girlfriends
not good enough for me

MORNING WALK

in the jammed park
between   veined   the cars
and dogs that pee next to
puddles of splashy water
the ground strewn
with conkers

I smoke cigars
in the meagre artificial light
of shortening days

people get onto buses
the windows steam up in
the breath of coats

the trees sag with starlings
from people's faces one reads
if only there was a war

and there the shop
where we sat on sundays
is shut   but
with a new interior

everything is dark and wet
with ink

everything moves on
the usual way

here is autumn

headlights sniff
in splashing water
the scent of a leaf

POSTE RESTANTE

sometimes I peer into the crannies
of my soul

there behind the scenes hides
lisping lust
rustling rancour
malice   the glass
and the germ of every
ambition

somewhere my mother walks
who finds the child even in
the deepest darkness

under her hat
she wears a black bow
in her hair

so does one dispute dying

you who also know the dark well
does your mother look on too –
at the burrowing of the whole world
and every small button of your lover?

the parental home
has been engulfed

with the simmering of meat
on the gas ring

and rain that meanders
down mat-glazed panes

my father's hand placed
round her shoulder

I am worn to the bone
have to learn everything anew
become yet more insignificant

I was once asked the question
if I could kill someone

one day
I will post myself

my mother   who sees all
asks no questions   only
every day
anything new?

POEM FOR MY 49TH BIRTHDAY

the loneliness of objects
at evening in look-alike streets

the gnarled names
carved in trees

like the painted empty space
next to widows
in their twin beds

or think of the dark silence
of the musician at the wedding

the smell of dead furniture
in second-hand shops

the feeling that someone
on the shoulders of someone
is watching too over the wall
of years

anyone alive also knows
the horror of marriages
the days that come
the days that go

like sex on a sunday morning
and butter that's good
for your cholesterol

the friend with his
all-of-a-sudden lesbian wife
then stays on nine more years

first love was there
then love was not there
then there was *not* love

thinking about
a face as of
a commercial the jingle
that sticks in your mind

suddenly along the
motionless river bank
my vigilant father walks
resistance is no virtue
but shows where the very own
storm is forming
I am the boy

say to those to come
that I will walk
in the dissembling present
towards the end
of the night
until the morning-red rain

THE SLEEPING BOY

the ice on the trolley bus wires sings us
to the dreamland of the river
over the bridge   a dark path
everything that I had lies on the other side
everything calls   everything hesitates

your street with the grey
photocopied houses
here people speak with rotting vowels
like lice of a local dialect

in the night of the multiple questions
the lingering of hours
mouth-watering on the sofa
as a farewell your hesitant cheek and
purple beading round my bike's handlebars

sometimes it feels like a betrayal
of my own 50 years   how it was

the gentle water of your eyes
divulges secrets
mine are still locked
in a journey towards apprehensive dreams

some day we will perhaps think
of when the first quarrel took place
and then think nothing more

any longer of your soft spot for africans
and my dark-sounding laugh

no more of the never-born child
the left-behind slippers
of an earlier love

and your words
why the bloody hell doesn't it work out?

the dislike of cigarettes
the hacking air
in your two-tone summer hair

*is your arm longer on this side
or mine shorter?*

beneath your gaze
my muscle tension   epidermis
is shattered

your belly of dancers from southern climes
in the early morning your blood-red lips
rise inaudibly

where behind the pussies of your eyes does the cat sit?

my mouth speaks like the flight of swallows
as summer draws near

and your pillow-smothered orgasm
because of the sleeping boy in the room next-door

A DISCOVERY OF WINGS

in the talkative summer
I live your scenario

that sweeps off into acrobatic
trips on my balcony

bear thrashes in your cesspool
of names –
the boyfriends of earlier years

only frontal nudity
lives in the present

like my absence
on each birthday
so does desire grow
like a waxing moon

but when you laugh
in nocturnal water meadows
I am susceptible to fear

I read in the river sand
us together
described as a footstep

both of us still have to
live in other places

like longing
for a more languid south

the mouthful love
that silently says
no you can have
yes is a word with six vowels

today it's over
so that you can write

separated behind
the firebreak of days

in the insatiable silence

I think of you
as the last word
of my name

FAREWELL

when we were even closer to each other's skin
neither poet   nor housewife
man and wife

I wanted to escape like breath
dew

and now that the spring falls short
like yesterday evening

I watch over my space as
dogs their yard

the decay of the frail machine
that gives and takes

I will remember you
fold dog-ears in the days' pages
wait

I toss like two persons
in a one-person bed

thinking of how you sat there and
the sweet kiss that quivered
above the tabletop

round your neck a string of family secrets
that I now snap one by one

I sang soldier's songs
in the lines of your hand
at the water's edge

the picnic in the shelter of the wood
keen like the deer further up

the weather wore summer clothes

it is not desire
that it is not

look at me then

that when I am not there
I am close to you too

what of me will reside in you?
what of you in me?

the reeking wound
of what is forfeited   the past
family and dreams

when the tramp disturbed our farewell
as if it was fitting
we still had to imagine
the sentences of the future

and your coat looked back at me

does anyone know what the empty
landscape looks like   the empty room?

someone looks
suddenly it exists

like the worn-out books
on the bookshelves
the fields fill up with
mortality

the ground mist that through the sun
rises into the sky
past branches
of black-indian ink

in this moment
in this emptiness eternity lies
because you record   look

the moment of the summer in your head
the smell of spring and late
autumn days   of a row of
jackets on hangers in a corridor
with high windows

the moment that your father
grasps your hand in the street

of a cap pistol
a swimming-bath girl
that pulls your willie

the moment that you no longer
give a dog and its grinding jaws
a wide berth

and that you break a tooth yourself

the moment of pleasure
of fugitiveness
of the salt on your lips

the moment of binding
and separation anxiety

the moment that you become gentle
that you as a milksop
are an outsider

the moment that you become your own
ambassador and vassal

that you see the *guernica*
and your own small war

that the porcelain breaks

WAGE WAR AGAIN

I've got to wage war again
urgently need to
wage war again

as when torn to pieces
by two women
who even possess your thoughts

(think of a civil war)

yet now everyone's dead
nothing is lost
I still remain who I am

got to wage war

no war of polemics
I wage war
just with myself
(watch out   someone may die)

you think you conquer the girl
and all turns out well

so you look for dates
from before it all happened

the ochre summers
when one was bored
when all was still full of promise

that you didn't know the word *sometimes*
would never become *often*
even fall silent

that some time later
– time still played its role
discreetly –
you came home badly drunk
your mother still up

that still later the others
the career   the girl
the car   and their money in the bank

that birthmarks
not yet malignant

and now   much older
I have to strike the children's flag

the scars bound up with
hefty bandages
terrain is still being won

I've got to wage war again
against a foe who is
waiting in the wings

smash the darkness to pieces
for concerned parents

ANNIVERSARY OF THE DEAD

at home there's a table for five
the plates still unbroken

outside the city the countryside
lies waiting as in old holidays

the quiet stream in summer
even then hinted at
raging winters

come   let me just make a call
to the dead

everyone sits in a circle
– the facade of small-talk –
I have broken with it

all uncles and aunts are still
from way before the war

that's the way with poets
they always call when everything's closed
and everyone gone

can I still speak to my mother?
and yes   that girlfriend is still there

or such a father who has achieved much
more that you ever assumed during
his life – said to him

do the neighbours there
still get
flowers on feast days too?

and do talkative aunts still
waste valuable time?

summer does not show itself
as a meadow full of breath
you touch your rod
in lonely rooms

nothing has changed
what do I know about life?

shall we go for a drive again
on sunday?   past tobacco barns
ditches   blossom   cherries and apples

there is no mercy
here the past lurks behind hedgerows
as never before

the reed bends slavishly as desire

a lament for slow-moving
searing days
when your parents were there

like birds that peck in
pitch-black furrows   and so destroying
the resentment of together

love sometimes scornful
as eyes
and the corn failing

I must urgently call
the dead

about the unforeseen scheme
of advancing life

relate everything now before
it becomes blurred

SO THERE ARE HOLES THEN

when you are young you still think
am I someone?

and then
will I become someone?

yes   I'll become someone

you travel with your father
to customers

in empty kitchens stand
pans on the stove

everyone is still light-footed

the south already starts
south of the city

past the hockey fields
where *she* is right-winger

but then the rot sets in

that you never feel at home
and always want ahead

your friends with brides fragile
as mother-of-pearl dolls
and triumphant their children

deserted from your youth
a somersault to later

the house is still standing
inhabited by strangers
and the trimmed hedge too
cut by the man in plus fours

before christmas the street smells
of scrapple

and there goes the hunchbacked friend
who avoided deportation
by becoming a catholic
patient

even the frail hockey girls have become
mothers with ample breasts

and you   yes you yourself   with your late love
that you can no longer shape

did you have to wait for that?

or was it better that you
in the moment?

the cruel present
smells increasingly of yesterday

you emigrate to
a city that never sleeps

all loved ones perish
calm and collected

such a cheerful lad
it's drizzling moths

have I become someone?

yes   so there are holes then
and no one – except yourself –
will fill them in

FINALE

now summer awakes
under a gutter
with cooing pigeons

the ironing smell
of always monday once more

an angry goblin
steps out of a book

there made of rags
lies dingdong the doll

twist-dress sisters stand laughing
on the edge of the ice-cold
inflatable water

one propagates via navels
neighbours stick their beaks
through the hole in the hedge

in the front garden
four shrubs as beatles

there too young
my father's jeep breaks

one talks of *jew's fat*
we say *sugar candy*
– because of the war –

upstairs grandma receives
the uncles with cigars

dolly mixture is a medicine
for distress

then a bit later avoiding the cracks
between paving stones

the walls throw the balls
to record heights

the pliable dreams
of balsa wood wake up

your basement is
nuclear-proof

on the bedside table stands a glass
of shamming lemonade

the retarded girl
is shrieking shrilly
behind a wall of years
is later incinerated in a bath

a rorschach test
on ink-black paper

a weightless swing
pinned onto a sheer blue sky

one says   in that last second
there is a replay of everything

London view, The sleeping boy, A discovery of wings, Farewell and *Finale* appeared in *Het liegend konijn 2013/2.*

An ordinary day appeared on 24 June 2015 in *De internet Gids* from the literary periodical *De Gids.*

Emigration and *On the other side of the water* are sections of the longer poem *On the other side of the water* and also appeared on 24 June 2015 in *De Internet Gids.*

London calling appeared in *Extaze 16/2015 no 4*

The word 'vroedvrouwpad' (midwife toad) in *Merciless recalling* comes from the serial *Axel*, which Pieter Thomassen wrote for the Holland Park Press Magazine.

The monsignor in *Merciless loving* is father Keith Barltrop, St. Mary of the Angels, Bayswater, London.

In this moment eternity lies refers to a statement made by David Hockney.

So there are holes then is dedicated to Ellen-Marie Vogel (Mönchengladbach, 1932 – Nijmegen, 2011).

My thanks to Dirk Vis of *De Gids* for the suggestion to use the line *I am the refrain of other people's lives* from the poem *On the other side of the water* as the title for the three poems accepted for the *Internet Gids*. This later led to it being adopted as the title of the collection.

Arnold Jansen op de Haar (Nijmegen, 1962) moved from Arnhem to London in 2014, where he works as an editor for Holland Park Press. His poems have appeared, among other places, in the periodicals *De Gids, Het liegend konijn, Extaze, Maatstaf, Zoetermeer* and *Passionate* and have been included in a number of anthologies, including *Komrij's Nederlandse Poëzie van de 19de t/m de 21ste eeuw in 2000 en enige gedichten* and in *Vrede is eten met muziek.* From 1999 to 2009 he was a columnist on *De Gelderlander.*

BIBLIOGRAPHY

Dutch

De koning van Tuzla, novel, De Arbeiderspers, 1999
Soldatenlaarzen, poetry, J.M. Meulenhoff, 2002
Van Jan Cremer tot Herman Koch, een literaire wandeling door Arnhem, non-fiction, Bibliotheek Arnhem, 2004
De twaalfde man, together with Jac. Toes, thriller, De Geus, 2006
Joegoslavisch requiem, poetry, reissue of *Soldatenlaarzen*, Holland Park Press, 2009
De koning van Tuzla, novel, reissue, Holland Park Press, 2009
Engel, novel, Holland Park Press, 2009
Het refrein van andermans leven, poetry, Holland Park Press, 2016

English

Yugoslav Requiem, poetry, Holland Park Press, 2009
King of Tuzla, novel, Holland Park Press, 2010
Angel, novel, Holland Park Press, 2011

John Irons studied Modern & Medieval Languages (German, French, & Dutch) at Cambridge University and completed his PhD *The Development of Imagery in the Poetry of PC Boutens* at the same university.

He worked as a senior lecturer at Odense University in Denmark. He has been a professional translator, from Danish, Swedish, Norwegian, Dutch, German and French to English, since 1987. He was awarded the NORLA translation prize for non-fiction in 2007.

John Irons has worked on a long and distinguished list of publications and he has been a translator for Poetry International Rotterdam since 1996. He has translated several of the leading authors and poets from the Low Countries including anthologies of Dutch-language poets Hugo Claus and Gerrit Komrij.

In 2015 Holland Park Press published *100 Dutch-Language Poems – From the Medieval Period to the Present Day*, selected and translated by Paul Vincent and John Irons. John Irons and Paul Vincent won the Oxford-Weidenfeld Translation Prize 2016 for this publication.

John Irons lives in Odense, Denmark.

http://johnirons.blogspot.co.uk/

Holland Park Press is a unique publishing initiative. Its aim is to promote poetry and literary fiction, and discover new writers. It specializes in contemporary English fiction and poetry, and translations of Dutch classics. It also gives contemporary Dutch writers the opportunity to be published in Dutch and English.

To

- Learn more about Arnold Jansen op de Haar
- Discover other interesting books
- Read our unique Anglo-Dutch magazine
- Find out how to submit your manuscript
- Take part in one of our competitions

Visit www.hollandparkpress.co.uk

Bookshop: http://www.hollandparkpress.co.uk/books.php

Holland Park Press in the social media:

http://www.twitter.com/HollandParkPres
http://www.facebook.com/HollandParkPress
https://www.linkedin.com/company/holland-park-press
http://www.youtube.com/user/HollandParkPress